GREAT LAKES
AND
GREAT SHIPS
AN ILLUSTRATED HISTORY FOR CHILDREN

John Mitchell & Tom Woodruff
for Matt, Andrew, Dudley and Mary

Suttons Bay Publications
301 St. Joseph - Box 361
Suttons Bay, Michigan 49682

LIBRARY OF CONGRESS CATALOG CARD NUMBER 91-65356
ISBN 0-9621466-1-7

In the heart of North America are five lakes so large they are known throughout the world as the Great Lakes.

The most important feature of the Great Lakes is their fresh water, a key ingredient of all life on earth. The five giant Lakes —named Superior, Michigan, Huron, Erie and Ontario — hold the world's largest supply of fresh water, enough to cover the United States nearly ten feet deep!

The land surrounding the Lakes is rich and varied, supporting many types of life. The abundant natural resources found around the Great Lakes are especially useful to people, who for thousands of years have prospered along their shores.

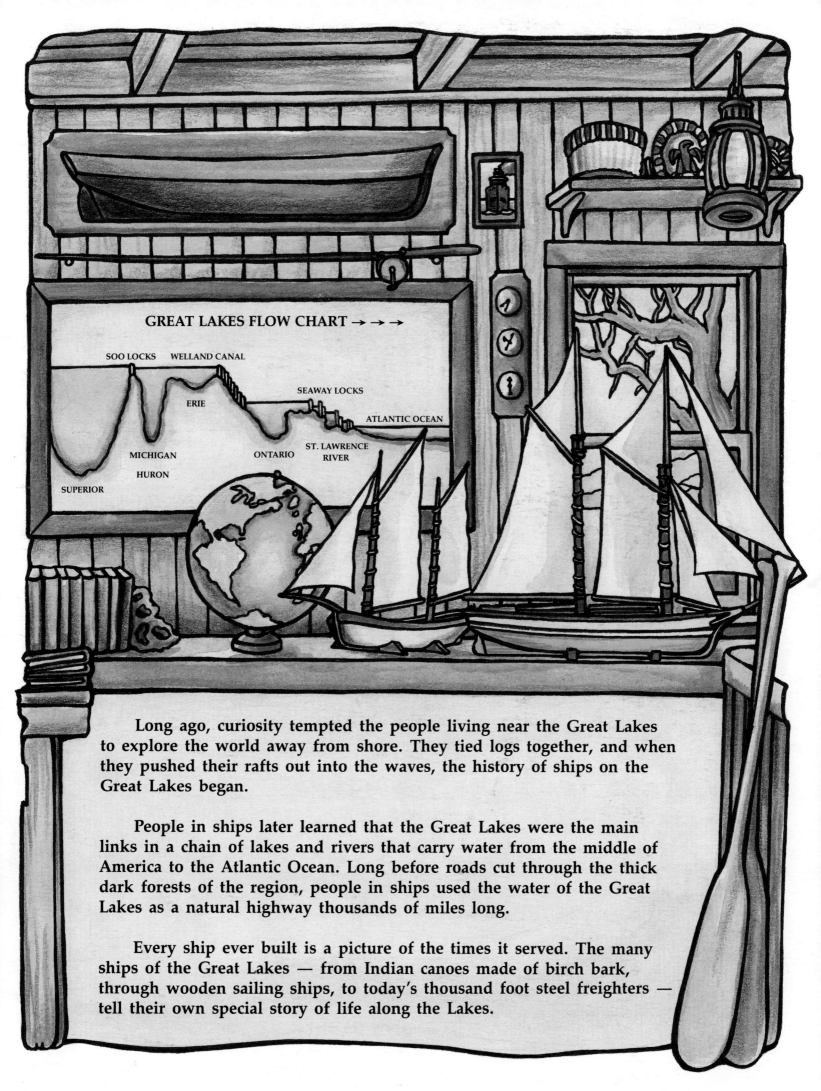

GREAT LAKES FLOW CHART → → →

SOO LOCKS   WELLAND CANAL

ERIE

SEAWAY LOCKS

ATLANTIC OCEAN

MICHIGAN

ST. LAWRENCE RIVER

HURON

ONTARIO

SUPERIOR

Long ago, curiosity tempted the people living near the Great Lakes to explore the world away from shore. They tied logs together, and when they pushed their rafts out into the waves, the history of ships on the Great Lakes began.

People in ships later learned that the Great Lakes were the main links in a chain of lakes and rivers that carry water from the middle of America to the Atlantic Ocean. Long before roads cut through the thick dark forests of the region, people in ships used the water of the Great Lakes as a natural highway thousands of miles long.

Every ship ever built is a picture of the times it served. The many ships of the Great Lakes — from Indian canoes made of birch bark, through wooden sailing ships, to today's thousand foot steel freighters — tell their own special story of life along the Lakes.

The earth is a very old planet which has changed on its surface many times. Only recently in the long life of the earth, the climate was much colder than it is today. Large parts of North America were covered with vast sheets of ice called glaciers.

The glaciers, many over a mile thick, pushed down from the north, destroying everything in their path. The weight of the advancing ice cut deep valleys in soft soil and crushed boulders to dust. In some places the earth's crust was scraped down to ancient rock, in others it was piled high with sand and gravel.

Ten thousand years ago, the earth warmed up and the glaciers retreated north. Some of the water they left behind filled low spots in North America and formed the five Great Lakes. The glaciers continued to melt. In time, the Lakes overflowed and drained east to the Atlantic Ocean, as they do today.

Fields of grass soon covered the land that was freed from the grip of the glaciers. Herds of mastodons and other big animals moved in to graze on the open pastures. Then came the earliest people, who roamed through the Great Lakes country in search of food. Survival from day-to-day depended on the success of the hunt.

Several skilled hunters armed with spears were needed to kill one of the huge animals living near the Lakes. Other people were needed to set up camp, to fish, and to care for the children. To make life easier, people began to work together in groups called tribes.

The early tribes worshipped the Great Lakes and the life-giving fresh water. For these people, the Lakes were a mysterious place, ruled by powerful spirits.

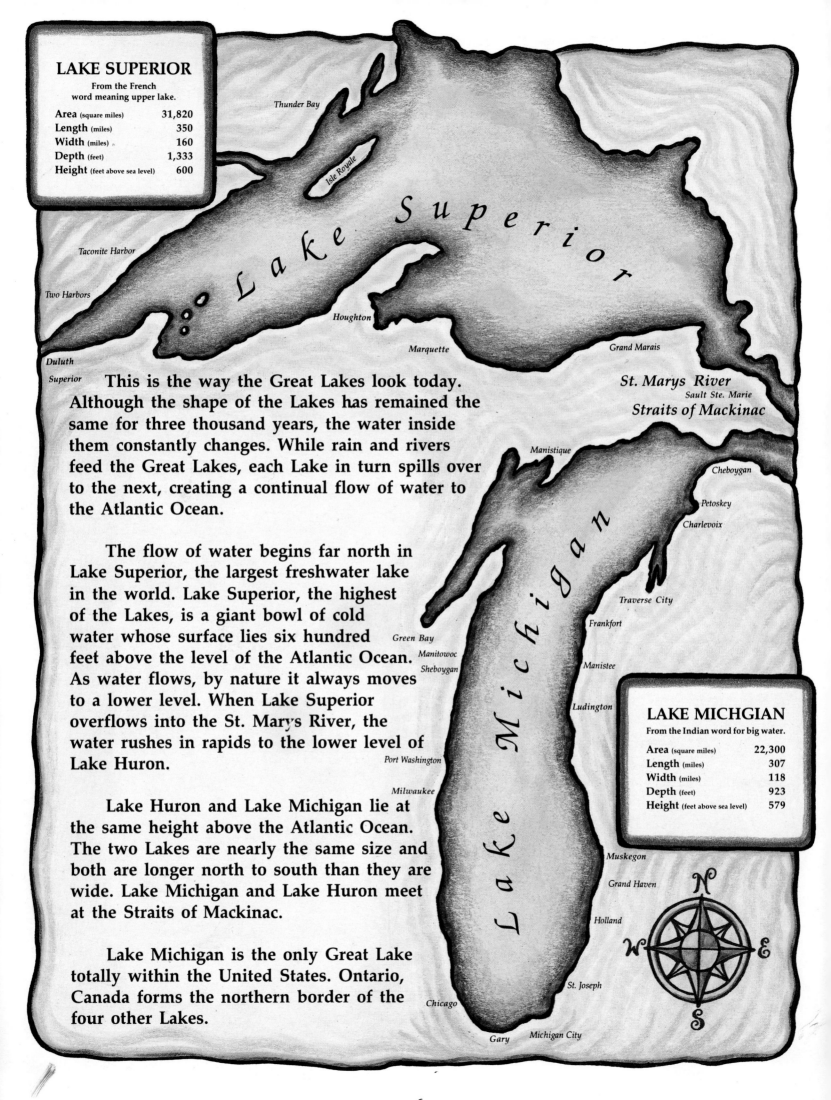

LAKE SUPERIOR

From the French
word meaning upper lake.

Area (square miles)	31,820
Length (miles)	350
Width (miles)	160
Depth (feet)	1,333
Height (feet above sea level)	600

Thunder Bay

Isle Royale

Lake Superior

Taconite Harbor

Two Harbors

Houghton

Duluth

Superior

Marquette

Grand Marais

St. Marys River

Sault Ste. Marie

Straits of Mackinac

Manistique

Cheboygan

Petoskey

Charlevoix

This is the way the Great Lakes look today. Although the shape of the Lakes has remained the same for three thousand years, the water inside them constantly changes. While rain and rivers feed the Great Lakes, each Lake in turn spills over to the next, creating a continual flow of water to the Atlantic Ocean.

The flow of water begins far north in Lake Superior, the largest freshwater lake in the world. Lake Superior, the highest of the Lakes, is a giant bowl of cold water whose surface lies six hundred feet above the level of the Atlantic Ocean. As water flows, by nature it always moves to a lower level. When Lake Superior overflows into the St. Marys River, the water rushes in rapids to the lower level of Lake Huron.

Lake Huron and Lake Michigan lie at the same height above the Atlantic Ocean. The two Lakes are nearly the same size and both are longer north to south than they are wide. Lake Michigan and Lake Huron meet at the Straits of Mackinac.

Lake Michigan is the only Great Lake totally within the United States. Ontario, Canada forms the northern border of the four other Lakes.

Traverse City

Frankfort

Green Bay

Manitowoc

Sheboygan

Manistee

Lake Michigan

Ludington

LAKE MICHGIAN

From the Indian word for big water.

Area (square miles)	22,300
Length (miles)	307
Width (miles)	118
Depth (feet)	923
Height (feet above sea level)	579

Port Washington

Milwaukee

Muskegon

Grand Haven

Holland

St. Joseph

Chicago

Gary   *Michigan City*

In time, the overflow of water from Lakes Superior, Michigan and Huron winds through Lake St. Clair and the Detroit River down to the level of Lake Erie. These four great Lakes are often called the Upper Lakes, for they lie on the same high shelf of earth. However, at the eastern edge of Lake Erie, the land takes a big step down. Here the water races through the Niagara River, then tumbles over Niagara Falls to the level of Lake Ontario three hundred twenty-five feet below.

The St. Lawrence River, which begins at the eastern end of Lake Ontario, is the last link in the chain of water flowing from the Great Lakes to the Atlantic Ocean.

The climate of the Great Lakes is ruled by the four seasons. During the winter, some areas of the Lakes and many harbors freeze over, ending navigation until the ice breaks up.

ST. LAWRENCE RIVER
(Seaway)

LAKE HURON
Named after the Huron Indians.

Area (square miles)	23,000
Length (miles)	206
Width (miles)	183
Depth (feet)	750
Height (feet above sea level)	579

LAKE ONTARIO
From the Indian word for beautiful water.

Area (square miles)	7,550
Length (miles)	193
Width (miles)	53
Depth (feet)	802
Height (feet above sea level)	245

LAKE ERIE
Named for an Indian tribe that once lived near the lake.

Area (square miles)	9,910
Length (miles)	240
Width (miles)	57
Depth (feet)	210
Height (feet above sea level)	570

Five thousand years ago, while Lake Superior was still being shaped by melting glaciers, a tribe known as the Old Copper Indians journeyed into the cold country to mine and shape copper. These early Indians hammered the soft red metal into spear points and axe heads, fish hooks and jewelry, and other items to use and trade.

The Old Copper Indians traveled between their many mines along Lake Superior in canoes dug out from logs. Using fire and copper tools, they burned and carved into a big tree trunk until a space was formed for passengers and cargo. When cold fall winds began to blow, they packed up their dug-out canoes and moved to warmer weather.

Long ago, the Old Copper Indians disappeared from the Great Lakes region, leaving behind only abandoned mines and copper tools as proof they ever existed.

Many different tribes rose to power during the long history of Indians in the Great Lakes region. Most tribes were nomadic, changing their homes with the changing seasons. All found that moving about in small open boats was easier than fighting their way through the thick forests inland.

Five hundred years ago, Great Lakes Indians built beautiful canoes from the bark of birch trees and other natural materials. The birch-bark canoes were strong yet light, and could cut through river rapids or glide along the shore with ease.

The Indians used their bark canoes in the same way people use automobiles today. The lakes and rivers were the highways connecting the many hunting, fishing and Indian trading centers along the Great Lakes.

In 1492, Christopher Columbus sailed from Europe, a land separated from North America and the Indians by the huge Atlantic Ocean. Before Columbus crossed the Atlantic and found the New World, the people living in the two far-away places knew nothing of each other.

The people of Europe were restless and curious about the world outside their own. The news of Columbus' discoveries stirred them to action. Several European nations built sailing ships tough enough to cross the Atlantic Ocean.

The nations of France and England, enemies in Europe, carried their fight across the ocean and began their long struggle for control of the Great Lakes.

The French claimed the coast where the mighty St. Lawrence River empties the waters of the Great Lakes into the Atlantic Ocean. In 1544, a Frenchman named Jacques Cartier was the first to explore the St. Lawrence, leading three ships up the wide river.

A thousand miles inland from the ocean, the St. Lawrence River narrows, and the force of the current stopped Cartier's ships. Cartier failed at his mission, for like many early explorers of America, he was looking for a water route to the rich country of China. However, the water route he followed would lead future Frenchmen into the heart of the even richer Great Lakes region.

The Frenchman, Samuel de Champlain, began the first exploration of the Great Lakes. In 1608, he journeyed up the St. Lawrence River and built a fort at a site he named Quebec. Then Champlain sent scouts deep into the unknown territory. The scouts traveled by water in birch-bark canoes. They lived in Indian camps and learned their ways. The reports they sent back to Champlain described for the first time the vast Great Lakes region.

While mountains slowed the English advance inland from the Atlantic coast, French scouts in canoes used the St. Lawrence River as a highway to explore all of the five Great Lakes. They found a wild area of dark forests, dotted with lakes, cut by rivers, and ruled by four different Indian nations.

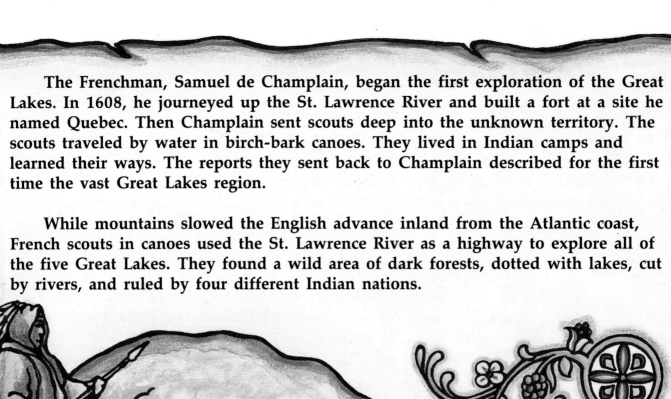

The Huron Indians farmed and hunted the land around the Lake that now bears their name. To the north and west of Lake Huron were the Algonquins, the people of three tribes united by the same language and religion. Around Lake Ontario and to its north lived the Iroquois, a nation of five tribes sworn by treaty not to fight against each other. The Sioux roamed the lands west of the Great Lakes.

Though the Indians grew some of their food, most tribes also depended on their large hunting grounds for survival. The tribal boundaries often changed as each Indian nation fought to control a bigger piece of the Great Lakes region.

IROQUOIS

Quebec

ATLANTIC OCEAN

Lake Ontario

The hundreds of rivers that flow into the Great Lakes were home to many beaver. For centuries, the Indians took from the rivers only the animals they needed for food and clothing. In Europe, where furs were scarce, coats and hats made from the beautiful fur of the beaver quickly became popular.

In trade for the furs, Europeans offered the Indians tools that made their work easier. Sharp metal knives cut better than Indian stones and shells. Bows and arrows were no match against deadly rifles. Indian hunters began to trap as many beaver as they could find, using their bundles of furs like money.

14

The Indians trapped beaver during the cold Great Lakes winters, when the fur of the animals grew the thickest. As soon as the ice melted, rugged men, called voyageurs, paddled many miles to meet with wilderness traders and carry their furs to market. Each year, the voyageurs built longer and stronger canoes to carry more furs. Often hundreds of canoes traveled together, and the songs and laughter of the voyageurs echoed through the quiet country.

At the same time, Catholic missionaries journeyed into the Great Lakes country and preached to the Indian tribes living there. The missionaries' carefully written journals of life and times among the tribes were widely read in Europe, inspiring others to come to the Great Lakes region.

In 1679, the Frenchman La Salle and his soldiers built the *Griffon*, the first ship to sail the Great Lakes.

On the first voyage, LaSalle sailed the *Griffon* west along Lake Erie, up Lake Huron, then across Lake Michigan to Wisconsin. Here the ship was loaded with furs. LaSalle then left to explore on shore, sending the *Griffon* off with the valuable cargo.

The *Griffon* sailed away and was never seen again. What happened to the ship is still a mystery today.

The bateau was a special type of wooden boat built to carry heavy loads of furs along the Great Lakes.

Made from a tough blend of oak and cedar wood, the bateau could bump down rocky rapids that would tear birch bark to pieces. On lakes, a sail could be raised to catch the wind. The center of the boat was made wide for cargo, and the bow and stern narrowed to points for better steering.

In 1701, a Frenchman named Cadillac built a fort near the river that connects Lake Huron to Lake Erie. He called the place Detroit. The French now had a string of forts along the Great Lakes, and fleets of bateaux and canoes could pass safely all through the region.

French forts along the Great Lakes depended on the water route along the St. Lawrence River to the Atlantic Ocean. Through this route came the soldiers, settlers and supplies needed to hold the vast area.

Lake Ontario is separated from the upper Great Lakes by mighty Niagara Falls. The most eastern of the Lakes, it was also the first where the English challenged the French in their long struggle to control the rich Great Lakes fur trade. Preparing for a war that was sure to come, the English launched the *Oswego* into Lake Ontario in 1755, one of the first sailing ships on the Lakes since the *Griffon*. The ship and its twelve cannons were a sign of growing English power.

When war erupted between the two countries a year later, the English concentrated their forces on driving the French out of the Great Lakes region.

In the spring of 1759, a fleet of English ships sailed up the St. Lawrence River and attacked Quebec, the center of French power.

Quebec was built on a tall rock wall rising from a riverbank. English ships commanded by General Wolfe controlled the river, but his troops could not capture the fort. A change in the color of leaves signaled the approach of winter. If the French Governor Montcalm could hold out for a few more weeks, the weather would force General Wolfe to withdraw his ships or have them trapped in ice.

One night, a small group of English soldiers captured a pathway up the cliffs. At daybreak, the two great armies clashed. French forces were soon defeated. Both Montcalm and Wolfe lost their lives in the battle. When the war ended four years later, the French surrendered their entire claim on the Great Lakes to the English.

Twenty years after defeating the French, the English lost a war to their rebellious American colonists. A new country, the United States of America, was born. The Great Lakes colonies of Pennsylvania and New York were two of the original thirteen states.

Although there was little fighting in the area, the war-weary English gave the United States the land south of the Great Lakes. This huge piece of wilderness was called the Northwest Territory. Later, the Territory would be divided into the states of Ohio, Illinois, Indiana, Michigan, Wisconsin and part of Minnesota. However, peace in the Territory did not last.

Disputes between England and the United States in the Great Lakes region were one of the causes of the War of 1812. On land, a series of American defeats soon allowed the English to control most of the Great Lakes.

20

The turning point of the War of 1812 came in a naval battle fought on Lake Erie. English warships attempting to carry supplies to troops were sighted by the American commander, Oliver Hazard Perry, who swung his ships into action.

Fighting at close range, Perry's ship, the *Lawrence*, was splintered by cannon shot and scorched by fire. Perry changed ships, fought on, and won the fierce battle. Perry sent his commanders the famous message, "We have met the enemy and they are ours . . ."

At the end of the War of 1812, England and the United States agreed never again to allow armed fleets on the Great Lakes. This historic treaty endures today, and the Great Lakes are part of the peaceful border between two free nations, the United States and Canada.

Two hundred years of fur trading brought Europeans to all parts of the Great Lakes. However, away from the few forts and trading posts, the land around the Lakes remained unsettled. The forests were ancient hunting grounds, entered only with the Indians' permission.

After the fighting between the United States and England ended, the Indian tribes slowly lost control of their lands. Word spread of peace in the beautiful Great Lakes region and more people took the chance and settled on Indian territory.

In 1818, the steamship, *Walk-In-The-Water*, traveled from Lake Erie to Detroit. The paddle-wheeled ship was the first modern, machine-powered vessel to journey above Niagara Falls. The *Walk-In-The-Water* was welcomed by settlers as a sign the Great Lakes wilderness was being tamed.

There was no easy way for pioneers to reach the Great Lakes from the Atlantic coast. The few wagon roads through the wild country were full of potholes and tree stumps. Dangerous rapids in the St. Lawrence River and Niagara Falls prevented big ships from reaching the Great Lakes from the Atlantic Ocean. Settlement west was slowed.

To solve the problem, the State of New York built the Erie Canal. Completed in 1825, the three hundred sixty mile long Erie Canal was an instant success. Canal boats pulled along by horses made the trip from the Atlantic to Lake Erie faster, cheaper, and easier than it had ever been before. New York City, where the trip to the Erie Canal began, became the world's gateway to America. The town of Buffalo, New York, where the Erie Canal met Lake Erie, grew from a sleepy outpost to the busiest port on the Great Lakes.

By the 1830's, stories of the rich land surrounding the Great Lakes were well known to the poor of Europe. Life in Europe offered them little freedom and few opportunities, while the chance for a new life in America filled them with hope. Entire families boarded ships and left Europe for America.

The people coming to America were called immigrants. Many of the immigrants heading for the Great Lakes traveled from the Atlantic coast through the Erie Canal. Ships then carried them from Lake Erie to the fertile land along Lakes Huron and Michigan. Each new steamship was built larger than the last to keep up with the increased number of travelers on the Great Lakes.

Chicago, Milwaukee, and other port towns grew quickly. In these frontier towns, immigrants first bought what they needed to start a farm. Later they arranged to ship their crops east to waiting markets. Everyone prospered. Working together, farmers and shippers made the Great Lakes region one of the largest food producers on earth.

In 1846, the beautiful wooden ship, *Phoenix*, was built for Great Lakes passenger trade. The speedy, one hundred fifty-five foot steamship was one of the first to use modern propellers instead of paddlewheels. The *Phoenix* took only ten days to travel from Lake Erie, through Lake Huron, to ports along Lake Michigan.

In late November 1847, the immigrants aboard the *Phoenix* were glad to be nearing the end of their voyage. They knew that over the years, November's icy storms had sunk many ships. Now, after traveling thousands of miles, the shores of Wisconsin were only a few miles away.

Suddenly the engine room of the ship burst into flames. Fire spread quickly along the wooden decks. People rushed from their cabins, but there were only two small lifeboats aboard. By the time the *Phoenix* burned to the waterline, two hundred people had died.

Whether powered by steam or sail, all Great Lakes ships of the 1850's were made of wood. The forests surrounding the Great Lakes provided the perfect materials for wooden shipbuilding. The ships took shape at the edge of the forests, where carpenters chose the best trees for the job. Tough oak was used for ribs and planks and tall pine trees for masts. The strong straight wood was the envy of shipbuilders throughout the world.

At this time, there were many more sailing ships than steamships working the Lakes. The big wooden ships, often designed and built by their captains, silently roamed the Lakes in search of cargo. Unlike steam-powered ships, their speed always depended on the amount of wind in their sails.

While steamships specialized in carrying passengers, sailing ships hauled the plows, wheels, nails and other supplies needed by western pioneers. They sailed back full of wheat, wood and other products from the frontier.

The most popular sailing ships of the 1850's, called schooners, were designed for speed and quick handling of cargo. The schooner, *Challenge*, launched from a Wisconisn shipyard in 1852, became the model for many ships of the Great Lakes sailing fleet.

The wooden hull of the ninety foot *Challenge* was wide across the middle for cargo and thin at the ends. The bow was specially shaped to cut through waves. The two pine masts of the schooner were nearly as tall as the ship was long. Angular sails swung out of the way when loading began and were easier to handle than square sails. The *Challenge* also had a shallow draft and did not need deep water to reach the docks of most towns.

During the shipping season, thousands of schooners spread their sails to the wind and carried the weight of the Great Lakes' trade. Together the beautiful sailing ships played an important part in supplying the early farm settlements around the Lakes.

Long cold winters and poor soil kept most people out of the Lake Superior region. Farmers could not feed their families from land where most crops failed. It seemed the land surrounding the northern Lake would stay wild forever.

However, in 1841, the geologist, Douglass Houghton, found large deposits of copper in Michigan's Upper Peninsula. Mountains of iron ore were later discovered nearby. America's first great mining rush began, and prospectors raced to Lake Superior's shores for their chance to strike it rich.

Ship traffic from Lake Superior to the lower Lakes was blocked by wild rapids of the St. Marys River. Here, the water of Lake Superior quickly drops twenty-two feet to the level of Lake Huron. Large ships trying to run the rapids were broken to pieces. Heavy metal cargo had to be unloaded, carried past the rapids, and then reloaded into ships waiting below.

A special canal with a gate, called a lock, was built to bring ships safely around the rapids of the St. Marys River. Completed in 1855, the lock at Sault St. Marie gently carried ships from one lake level to another. The ninety-one foot *Columbia*, loaded with a cargo of iron, was the first ship to pass down through the lock to Lake Huron.

Earlier, Canada had built a series of locks called the Welland Canal. These locks worked like steps in a staircase and carried ships from Lake Erie to Lake Ontario by going around Niagara Falls. With locks around Niagara Falls and the rapids of St. Marys River, big ships could now travel freely between all the Great Lakes.

Steamships and schooners carried metal from Lake Superior docks to towns along the southern Lakes. Here new factories made wheels and engines, guns and wire, and hundreds of other metal products. In many places along the Lakes, people began to work in factories instead of on farms.

In 1861, the Civil War split the United States apart — North against South — in the fight over slavery. President Lincoln led the North in the struggle for a united country with freedom for all its people. None of the eight Great Lakes states allowed slavery. All sent soldiers and supplies to war against the South.

The weapons of the Civil War — cannons and rifles, bullets and bayonets — were made of metal. The North relied on a steady stream of ships carrying metal ore from Lake Superior mines to weapon factories along the Great Lakes. The South, however, depended on farming and had few factories or mines.

During the Civil War, a prison for captured Southern soldiers was built on Johnson Island in Lake Erie. The prison was guarded by the gunboat *Michigan*. In the fall of 1864, a group of Southerners plotted to ambush the *Michigan* and free the soldiers held on the prison island.

The steamship, *Philo Parsons*, was making regular stops along Lake Erie when it was hijacked by Southerners and driven to Johnson Island. That night, the hijackers waited for a signal that the *Michigan* had also been captured. However, the plot was discovered. The *Michigan* stood ready for action. The hijackers steered the *Parsons* into the darkness and fled.

The next year, the North defeated the South, and the United States was again one nation. In 1867, the British colonies to the north of the United States formed their own nation, the Dominion of Canada.

PHILO PARSONS

Between 1830 and 1870, Chicago, Illinois grew from a small Indian camp to one of the largest cities on the Great Lakes. Located on the southern shore of Lake Michigan, busy Chicago was the last stop for ships headed west. It was also the closest port for frontier farmers to ship crops east. Many passengers arriving in Chicago found work and stayed.

During the summer of 1871, very little rain fell on the Great Lakes region. In Chicago, hot air curled from the roofs of tightly packed wooden buildings and horses pawed the dry dusty streets. People worried and prayed for rain.

One August afternoon, a fire started in a barn. Strong winds fanned the flames and soon Chicago was burning. City blocks blazed out of control and the heat caused ships at anchor to burst into flames. People ran for their lives. For two days the city burned and, in the end, Chicago lay in ashes.

For thousands of years, huge forests darkened much of the Great Lakes countryside. Pioneers used a few trees to build their farms, then cut and burned the rest to let in light for crops. After the Civil War, more and more people moved to the Great Lakes region and built new houses and towns. Lumber became valuable and workers, called lumberjacks, began to cut trees for their wood.

The white pine tree was the king of the forests. The beautiful pines often grew five feet wide and one hundred fifty feet tall. The wood from the white pine was strong, yet light and easy to cut. These trees were first to fall to the lumberjack's axe.

Lumberjacks filled rivers with floating logs. Sawmills were built where the rivers widened to meet the Great Lakes. Outside the mills, stacks of cut wood crowded the docks. Dozens of wooden steamships, called lumber hookers, carried the wood to the towns springing up along the Lakes.

By the 1870's, ships faced tough competition from the many railroads that crossed the Great Lakes region. Unaffected by storms or the change in seasons, trains proved the best way to transport many types of cargo. However, for many people, travel by train could not match the beauty and adventure of a steamship ride along the Lakes.

The steamship, *India*, was one of many ships that carried passengers and cargo across the Great Lakes. When launched in 1871, the *India* was one of the largest and most luxurious ships ever built. Cabins were finished with polished wood, crystal chandeliers swayed from the ceilings, and meals were served in elegant dining halls. Below deck, the modern iron hull of the *India* was packed with cargo.

For over thirty years, the beautiful *India* cruised between Buffalo, New York on Lake Erie, and Duluth, Minnesota on the western edge of Lake Superior.

Over the years, steamships grew larger and their engines more dependable. Sailing ships remained at the mercy of the wind and weather. As Great Lakes fleets grew, more and more captains chose steam over sail to power their ships.

The *David Dows* was built to show that large, fast sailing ships were a match for modern steamships. Launched from an Ohio shipyard in 1881, the two hundred seventy foot *Dows* was the largest sailing ship ever to work the Great Lakes. Five tall masts and big sails made the speedy *Dows* the talk of the Lakes.

However, the *Dows* proved too big for her own good. The heavy sails took a long time to set and in a high wind the ship was difficult to steer. The busy shipping season crowded the Lakes, and the hard to handle *Dows* was soon involved in several collisions. Eight years after launching, the *Dows* sank in a November storm on Lake Michigan.

Storms on the Great Lakes have sunk thousands of ships. Before the age of modern radio communications, all ships were at the mercy of sudden changes in weather common on the Great Lakes. Waves rose without warning and heavy winds pushed ships toward dangerous shallows. Many ships were broken to pieces within sight of land.

In the early days of Great Lakes shipping, surviving a shipwreck was up to the skill and luck of each sailor. Few towns had rescue plans ready to help ships in trouble. Then in 1871, the United States Lifesaving Service was formed. Twenty-nine lifesaving stations were built at dangerous spots along the Lakes.

The crews of the lifesaving stations were trained and equipped for near-shore rescue. Whenever possible, brass cannon shot ropes to stranded ships. Then lifesavers hauled survivors to shore in baskets called breeches buoys. When needed, brave rescuers took to the stormy waters in surfboats. Every station has its own stories of shipwrecks and heroes.

The Lifesaving Service became part of the U.S. Coast Guard in 1915.

Fishing has always been an important source of food and sport for people living along the Great Lakes. Indians were expert fishermen. For centuries, tribes would gather along the St. Marys River for a fall feast of whitefish. Skilled Indians worked the river rapids with scoop nets and quickly filled their birch-bark canoes.

One hundred years ago, many ships searched the Great Lakes for fish. Small open sailing vessels, called Mackinaw boats, pulled lines and nets through the blue water. The beautiful wooden boats were often built by the fishermen who sailed them. Later, machine-powered ships, which were covered against the cold of the Great Lakes, became popular.

The fishing fleets were run by families who depended on the catch for their livelihood. On a good trip, whitefish and lake trout were brought up in nets by the ton. The fine tasting fish were served in homes and restaurants throughout North America. The fishermen taught their skills to their children, and where the fishing was good, harbors filled with docks, boats, and nets of the trade.

In 1882, the iron-hulled *Onoko* was launched from a Cleveland, Ohio shipyard. Designed to carry large loads of iron ore, the *Onoko*, with long rows of cargo hatches, was the shape of ships to come.

By 1890, manufacturing centers along the Great Lakes had mastered the skill of producing iron and steel products from iron ore. Ships made of metal were being built longer and stronger than those made of wood. By then, steam-powered saws had also cut most of the Great Lakes forests to lumber. As the forests neared their end, iron ore mined in the Lake Superior region replaced wood as the chief material in shipbuilding.

The success of big metal ships powered by steam engines drove wooden sailing ships from the Great Lakes. Many of the proud sailing vessels spent their last years being towed as barges behind a steam-powered tug.

A fleet of strange looking steamships, called whalebacks, were the first ships on the Great Lakes made entirely of steel.

Whalebacks were designed by the experienced ship captain and inventor, Alexander McDougall, for work on the Great Lakes. At first people laughed at the sight of the whalebacks, which looked like today's submarines. But the ships proved to be dependable haulers. Rounded sides let wind and water slip off the decks. Rows of hatches made loading and unloading easier. Some whalebacks were over four hundred feet long — twice the size of most wooden ships.

During the 1890's, more than forty whalebacks were launched from Lake Superior shipyards in Duluth, Minnesota and Superior, Wisconsin. Their success sped the change from wood to steel ships.

A century of rapid settlement along the Great Lakes changed many quiet villages into busy port cities. The first wave of pioneers survived by farming the rich soil. However, by 1900, the Great Lakes region was famous for manufacturing. Factory jobs and good pay drew farmers as well as immigrants to the cities by the Lakes.

Ships were the best way to carry large loads of the same kind of cargo to people and factories along the Great Lakes. A single ship could carry the harvest of thousands of acres of farmland. Another ship stopping at a Lake Superior dock could quickly load the iron ore from hundreds of train cars.

The natural beauty of the many harbors gave way to the workers and machinery needed to handle the loads of more and bigger ships.

By the turn of the century, many steamships competed for passengers traveling between Great Lakes ports. Rivalry between captains and ships grew as each steamer claimed to be the biggest, fastest, and best equipped on the Lakes.

In 1901, the *Tashmoo* and the *City of Erie*, both over three hundred feet long, were two of the most popular steamers on Lake Erie. To settle arguments over which paddle-wheeled ship was fastest, the owners agreed to a race. Thousands of people lined the docks to cheer for their favorite.

The lighter *Tashmoo* took an early lead, at times reaching speeds of twenty-five miles an hour. Near the end of the one hundred mile course, the *City of Erie* crept up and passed the *Tashmoo*, winning the famous race by less than a minute.

The discovery of iron in Michigan during the 1840's was followed by even bigger strikes in Minnesota in the 1880's. Factories were guaranteed a steady supply of iron ore and a growing market for steel products. Rather than hire ships to carry ore, companies that made iron ore into steel began to buy their own ships.

The first Great Lakes freighter over six hundred feet long was made for a steel company in 1906. Soon dozens of giant ships brought iron ore down Lake Superior to factories on the southern edge of the Lakes. Every year, new ships set records for their size and the amount they could carry. As fast as machines could unload the ships, their cargo of iron ore was taken to mills and turned into steel.

In 1909, Henry Ford opened a factory in Michigan that produced hundreds of Model T automobiles every day. Each automobile used nearly a thousand pounds of steel parts. The steel fleets grew. Big ships full of iron ore crossed the Lakes from spring until the shipping lanes froze.

The automobile changed America. Roads were improved and people in cars traveled from town to town quickly, and on their own schedule. The Great Lakes region led the world in automobile production, and the popularity of cars all but ended passenger travel on the Lakes. Most new ships were designed to carry large loads of iron, wheat, coal and other bulk cargoes.

Ferries were one type of lake transportation that prospered with the coming of the automobile. Since the Civil War, railroad car ferries were an important link on the rail system. Rather than lay hundreds of miles of tracks around lakes and rivers, whole trains were loaded on ferries and carried across the water.

By 1915, many people owned automobiles. Touring the countryside became a favorite pastime. At the time, only a few bridges had been built for the new machines. In ports along Lakes Michigan and Erie, and in other places where a narrow body of water caused a long detour by land, automobiles lined up alongside trains for a place on the ferries.

During World War I, many ships were needed to carry soldiers and supplies to Europe. By then, the Great Lakes fleet was one of the largest in the world. However, most big freighters could not reach the Atlantic Ocean from the Great Lakes.

The locks of the Welland Canal, which connect Lake Erie to Lake Ontario by going around Niagara Falls, were only two hundred seventy feet in length. Locks around the rapids of the St. Lawrence River were also smaller than most of the big new ships working the Great Lakes.

To help supply the war in Europe, Great Lakes shipyards built a fleet of smaller ships. These ships could pass through the locks and travel the oceans. After the war, many of the sturdy ships returned to the Lakes. Some carried freight. Others rusted at anchor or were cut up for their steel. At the outbreak of World War II, the ships that survived were again called to salt water duty.

During the 1950's, the Great Lakes region led the world in manufacturing. The quality metal products made in the region were respected as the best that could be built.

The Great Lakes in the 1950's were also home to the largest construction projects in the world. The five mile long Mackinaw Bridge, which links the Upper and Lower Peninsulas of Michigan, was completed in 1957. A year later, the seven hundred twenty-nine foot *Edmund Fitzgerald* was launched, then the largest ship on the Lakes. The St. Lawrence Seaway opened in 1959. The five large locks of the Seaway let ships the size of the *Fitzgerald* pass all the way from Lake Superior to the Atlantic Ocean.

In the past, the icy storms of November had sunk many ships and closed the Lakes for the season. But by 1950, Coast Guard ice breakers kept shipping lanes open through December. Many people believed the big ships could ride out the worst of weather. Then in November, 1975, a big storm on Lake Superior took the *Fitzgerald* and her cargo of iron ore to the bottom.

In 1900, thirty million people lived in the Great Lakes region. At the time, few ships were longer than four hundred feet. By 1971, when the first one thousand foot ship was launched, the population of the Great Lakes area had grown to over eighty million people.

As more and more people settled near the Lakes, many natural resources were used up to meet their needs. Furs, trees, metals, and other natural treasures were sold as fast as ships could deliver them to market.

In recent times, the greatest resource of the Great Lakes — the pure fresh water — has been threatened. Marine life from the oceans has entered the Lakes through ship channels and upset the balance of nature. Years of dumping chemicals from factories and waste from cities has in some places turned the water from blue to brown. Fish have died and beaches have been closed.

Today, the clean-up of the Great Lakes has begun. New laws guard the water from further pollution. Scientists study ways to better balance the needs of people and nature. More people understand that the Lakes and their tremendous supply of fresh water are a global treasure, one that must be protected for the good of all life on earth.

While big freighters continue to haul cargo, new fleets of sailboats carry people out to enjoy the Lakes. Fish have returned to waters where a short time ago there was no life. In the warm season, children gather on beaches for the simple pleasures of a summer day.

The future of the Great Lakes will soon be trusted to today's children. The decisions they make will write tomorrow's stories of the Great Lakes.